New Resolutions

Elena De Ceasare

Presentation by *BookLeaf Publishing*

Web: www.bookleafpub.com

E-mail: info@bookleafpub.com

ISBN: 9789357440998

First edition 2023

Leave You in 2022

When the clock strikes 12
and all confetti slowly begins its decent to the
ground
do not wait for me,
I will no longer be around.

Please understand
there is nothing you can do.
It is for my own healing
that I leave you 2022

Resolution

In this year I will...
no.
I this year I want to-
change. be better. be happy. be healthy. stick to
my promises. be independent. fall in love... with
myself. heal myself. quit my vices. be in shape.
eat better. practice self care. clean weekly. be
organized. save more. read more. do...
everything.

Hello Old Friend

Hello old friend,
I know we haven't talked in weeks, that is on
me. The crushing weight of my own thoughts
have begun suffocating me. Distance. That's one
thing. Mission accomplished. You needed space
and I needed to heal. You permit my writing of
letters, so you claim. And while on one hand I'm
inclined to believe you, your lack of enthusiasm
and response speaks volumes. Or does it?
Should it? Am I wrong for envisioning you
concocting some machiavellian plot to torment
me? Surely it is not true, but as the racing
thoughts in my mind make their rounds, they are
devoid of all logic and reason. So I apologize for
the way I operate... I promise I've been working
on it.

Nothing New

It's amazing how short a week can be when there
is nothing to do.
The days are bleak and mundane.
I have been reduced to factory settings.
Every blink feels like lifetime.
I forget what I ate for dinner.
I stop feeling anything.
I am numb to my own existence,
but at least I am no longer a stranger to it.

Routine

MONDAY
Wake up
Run
Shower
Work
Homework
Cook
Eat
Gym
Read
Sleep

TUESDAY
Wake up
Run
Shower
Work
Homework
Eat
Gym
Read
Sleep

WEDNESDAY
Wake up

Run
Shower
Work
Homework
Eat
Gym
Sleep

THURSDAY
Wake up
Run
Shower
Work
Homework
Eat
Sleep

FRIDAY
Wake up
Run
Shower
Work
Nap
Eat
Gym
Sleep

SATURDAY
Crash

SUNDAY
Catch-up on what was skipped

repeat.

Playing Pretend

When I was 5,
I was told I had an overactive imagination.
Like,
I wanted to be an Astronaut Veterinarian when I
grew up.
Or,
like...
I like to pretend.
Pretend I'm this amazing girl,
with infinite possibilities ahead of her.
Pretend I'm some incredible singer
when my brain goes into autopilot on the
freeway.
Pretend I'm a good person,
not someone who drove everyone away.
Pretend I'm the one who left for the better,
not the one left behind

Rose

The name my mother always called me:
Rosie.
And the sing-songy way the name rang from her
mouth,
Forever etched in my mind.
Maybe you'd like to know where it came from.
A cute story, sure.
But the name comes with a curse.

Mirror

Without saying words,
my mind runs rampant.
A black marker,
mentally outlining all the little things,
small imperfects,
flaws.
The baby fat.
The droopy eyelid.
The fat nose.
The broad man shoulders.
The acne scars.
As the scalpel of my disdain cuts deeper,
The bitchiness.
The awkwardness.
The fear.
The codependency.
The need to be loved.
The hatred.
The anger.
I am left with one conclusion:
I am bad.
I need to change.

For me

I realize now, I am my downfall. And I am the only one who can fix it. I cannot relay on others. I cannot ask them to help. Unconditional fidelity is the crutch. I loathe the products of actions, but forgiveness is amnesty, and somethings do not warrant forgiveness. Not yet. I need to change. Not to regain those I have lost, but for me. That is the only way change can last.

Curses

Maybe it's my fault.
I always wanted glasses as a kid.
Still do.
I just never realized the wish came true.
And then I was so dependent on the
Rose-colored lenses,
that I forgot I was wearing them.

FN Perfect

21 days,
That's all you have.
And you are determined,
but you are busy.
This has always been a hobby,
not a carrer.
It still is,
that hasn't changed.
No one will probably see this.
No one will probably read this.
You are too shy,
too anxious,
too...
hard on yourself.
22 years of being a perfectionist,
where has it gotten you?
Procrastination and regret.
Self-hatred and sleepless nights.
And yes, it will always get done,
but at what cost?
You can never be satisfied.
The perfect grade,
the standing ovation.
Never enough for you.
No matter how hard you try,

no matter how well you do,
you consider yourself a failure.
so please,
for once,
just let the words flow.
No one expects you to be Walt Whitman.
You are a beginner.
Just be proud of yourself.

Everlasting

P.
He was the one.
At 17 I was sure of it.
But after a 2 year battle,
I was the only one to feel that way.

Then I met N.
He was the one.
At 19 I was sure of it.
He bandaged the paper cuts P. left behind.
But as we both grew up,
we grew apart.
And the distance between us
felt longer than the 845 miles between us.

Then came J.
He was the one.
At 20 I was sure of it.
He bandaged the slits N. left behind.
It was easy.
It was normal.
It was... boring.
It was too adult, too fast.
So much love, but so much fear.
I'm sorry.

Last was B.
He was the one.
At 22 I was sure of it.
He tourniquet the gashes left behind.
My scars had reopened,
but he learned to sew to stitch me up.
And for once,
I felt healthy.
I felt safe.
I felt promise.
I guess... it wasn't the same for you,
not anymore.

I know now,
they were not the one,
but my love will transcend the time we were
together.

New Perspective

Two sides
that's what they say
I disagree
Life is not black and white.
There are not two sides to every story,
there are infinite.
We determine finality.
I shed the pink tint.
What is it really?
Put it into context.
Art is subjective.
I suppose life is the grandest performance art.
What a thought.

Happiness

Finally,
18 weeks clean.
The shakes subside
The last bead of sweat dropped
and I met the new me.
The rolling thunder and grayscale painted sky,
parted at last,
as gold rivers of sunlight tore the clouds apart.
And there it was.
I found the happiness after you
because I found it in myself.

The Night We Met

Today I went to our spot.
The cold, vacant diner on the inconvenient side
of a divided highway.
It was 2am on a Thursday and,
unlike the late Sunday morning breakfasts of
before,
no other customers were to be had.
And while I miss the shitty pancakes
overloaded with whipped cream,
all I could stomach was a coffee
lukewarm and black.
Bitter, sure, but thats how I drank it.
As did you--
or perhaps still do.
And it's funny.
Not overwhelmingly so,
but just enough
so that the corner of my mouth curls.
And all I can think is:
Dark chocolate.
I guess I was never too big a fan of sweets.

Thank You for Leaving

Thank you for being in my life.
You were a positive force,
I was the negative charge.
Thank you for playing your role.
As I broke,
You picked up the pieces.
Thank you for your time
I couldn't bare isolation,
You let me be around.
But most of all,
Thank you for leaving.
You needed you space,
I needed to grow.

One Day

One day, at approximately 7:29am
on one mild, Sunday morning
the rising sun will ignite the stain glass tint on
my window,
reflecting off the glitter, the warmth will pierce
my eyelid
as I will come out my hibernation.
A lifetime's worth of sleep
and maybe last year was all a bad dream.
I extend my arms out,
energizing my body again.
And for once I do not reach for your vacancy.
You do not cross my mind.
I am alone,
but on this day
and everyday henceforth,
I am whole.

Leave Me in 2023

Leave me in 2023.
The year will end,
and I will finally be free.
A year of growth,
has come and gone,
But my absence
must be prolonged.
Your return,
though anticipated,
is underserved.
So please leave me,
this time,
I need it for me.

www.ingramcontent.com/pod-product-compliance
Lightning Source LLC
LaVergne TN
LVHW050302200726
843509LV00015B/3113